(name)

# HAPPY BIRTHDAY TO ME!

## By ME, Myself

I wrote it! I drew it!

with a little help from my friend

# Dr. Seuss

Random House New York

ISBN 978-0-553-53719-2

Library of Congress Control Number: 2016948967

Printed in the United States of America

10 9 8 7 6 5 4 3 2 1

# HAPPY BIRTHDAY TO ME!

In Katroo, every year,
on the day you were born
They start the day right
in the bright early morn . . .

When I wake up
on my birthday this year,

I will be ____ years old.
<sub>number</sub>

I was born on _____ ____, _____
month         day        year

at _____,
time

in _____, ____.
city                      state

The Birthday Honk-Honker
hikes high up Mt. Zorn
And lets loose a big blast
on the big Birthday Horn.
And the voice of the horn
calls out as it plays:
"Wake up! For today
is your Day of all Days!"

# On my birthday, I want to get up:

as early as possible ☐

as late as I want ☐

never—I want to spend the whole day in bed! ☐

Then, the moment the Horn's
happy honk-honk is heard,
Comes a fluttering flap-flap!
And then comes THE BIRD!

That's him—the Great Birthday Bird! I colored him. ⬆

Whether your name is
Pete, Polly, or Paul,
When your birthday comes round,
he's in charge of it all.

If I could do ANYTHING
on my birthday, I would:

drive a race car ☐

eat ice cream all day ☐

fly to the moon ☐

go on a shopping spree ☐

sit under a tree and read ☐

spend the day at home in my pajamas ☐

swim with sharks ☐

_____ ☐

It's your Day of all Days!
It's the Best of the Best!
So don't waste a minute!
Hop to it! Get dressed!

# On my birthday, I'm going to wear:

something new and special ☐

something old and comfortable ☐

I have no idea! ☐

Here's a picture of me in my birthday outfit

"Today," laughs the Bird,
"eat whatever you want.
Today no one tells you
you cawnt or you shawnt."

# On my birthday,
# I want to eat these things:

circle the things you will eat

| | | |
|---|---|---|
| apples | dip | pizza |
| bacon | doughnuts | popcorn |
| baked beans | empanadas | pretzels |
| bananas | fish sticks | pudding |
| barbecue | French fries | salad |
| brownies | frozen yogurt | salsa |
| burgers | grapes | spaghetti |
| cake | grilled cheese | strawberries |
| candy | hot chocolate | tacos |
| cereal | hot dogs | tater tots |
| chicken nuggets | ice cream | tuna fish |
| chips | mac and cheese | waffles |
| cold cuts | nachos | watermelon |
| cookies | noodles | _____ |
| corn on the cob | oranges | _____ |
| cotton candy | pancakes | _____ |
| cucumbers | peanut butter and jelly | _____ |
| cupcakes | pineapple | _____ |

If we didn't have birthdays,
you wouldn't be you.
If you'd never been born,
well then what would you do?

If I was never born, I might be:

a fish ☐

a toad in a tree ☐

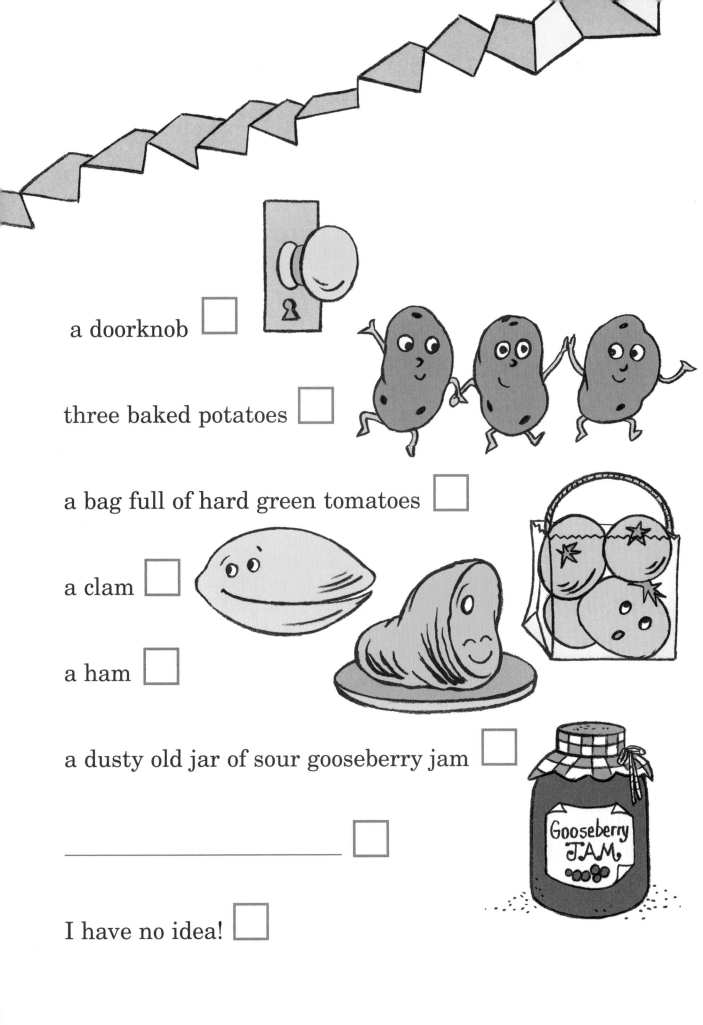

a doorknob ☐

three baked potatoes ☐

a bag full of hard green tomatoes ☐

a clam ☐

a ham ☐

a dusty old jar of sour gooseberry jam ☐

_____ ☐

I have no idea! ☐

# Everyone has a birthday!

## I asked my family and friends to write down theirs here:

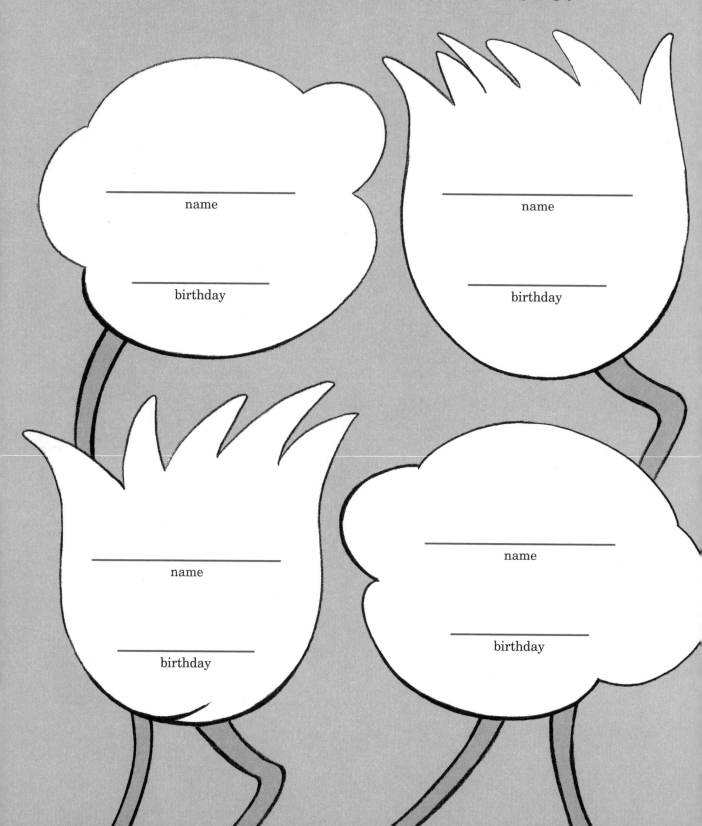

_____
name

_____
birthday

_____
name

_____
birthday

_____
name

_____
birthday

_____
name

_____
birthday

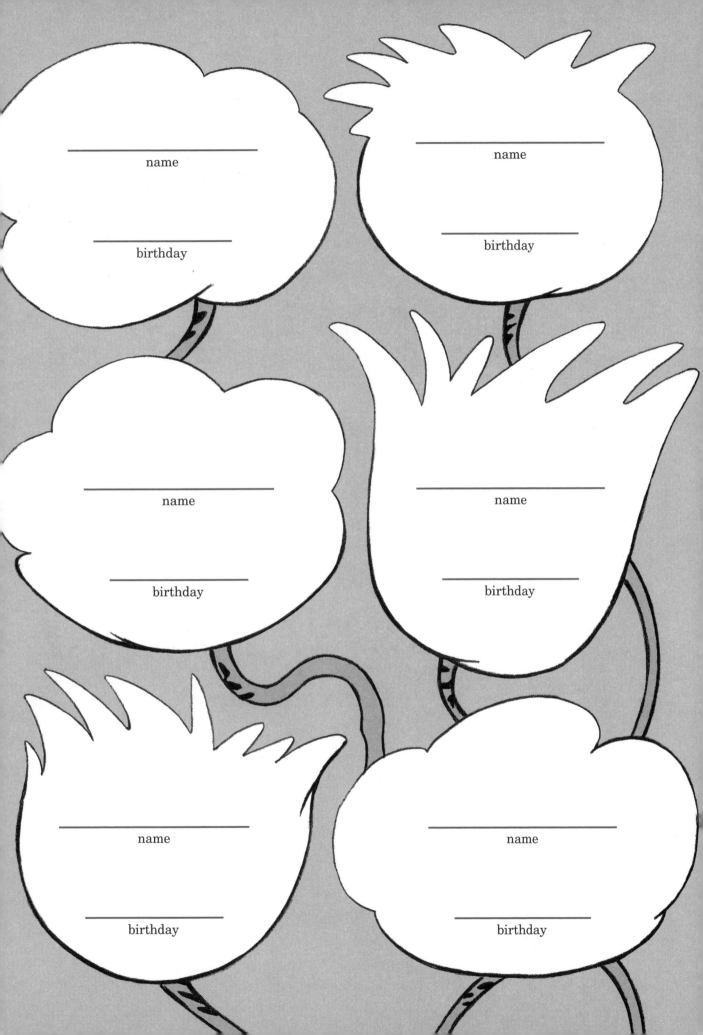

_____
name

_____
birthday

_____
name

_____
birthday

_____
name

_____
birthday

_____
name

_____
birthday

_____
name

_____
birthday

_____
name

_____
birthday

Shout loud
at the top of your voice,
"I AM I!
ME! I am I!
And I may not know why
But I know that I like it.
Three cheers!
I AM I!"

# Here are ten things
# I like about ME, myself:

1. _____

2. _____

3. _____

4. _____

5. _____

6. _____

7. _____

8. _____

9. _____

10. _____

The best-sniffing flowers
that anyone grows
We have grown to be sniffed
by your own private nose.

# I drew this flower ↙

It smells like _____.

# For Birthday luncheons, as a rule,
## We serve hot dogs, rolled on a spool.

**Follow the trail
of hot dogs to the
Mustard-Off Pools!**

START

Then, out of the water!
Sing loud while you dry!
Sing loud, "I am lucky!"
Sing loud, "I am I!"

say I have a beautiful voice ☐

sing along with me ☐

cover their ears ☐

run! ☐

My three favorite songs to sing are:

1. _____

2. _____

3. _____

A Present! A-ha!
Now what kind shall I give . . . ?
Why, the kind you'll remember
As long as you live!

The present I'd like most is

_____

I'd remember it as long as I live because

_____

_____

_____

Would you like a fine pet?
Well, that's just what you'll get.

If I could get a pet for my birthday,
I'd want a:

_____

cat

stuffed animal

horse

turtle

bird

lizard

hamster

gerbil

guinea pig

dog

fish

rabbit

snake

Today is your birthday!
You get what you wish.
You also might like a
nice Time-Telling Fish.

# If I had **three wishes,** I'd wish for:

1. _____

2. _____

3. _____

Your Big Birthday Party
soon starts to begin
In the finest Pal-alace
you've ever been in!

# I'd like a birthday party.

YES ☐          NO ☐

check one

# I'd like to have MY party HERE:

circle where you'd like your party to be

| | | |
|---|---|---|
| amusement park | haunted house | Pluto |
| aquarium | home | racetrack |
| backyard | horse show | restaurant |
| baseball game | ice cream shop | roller rink |
| basketball game | Katroo | skating rink |
| beach | lake | soccer game |
| bowling alley | mountaintop | swimming pool |
| circus | movie theater | tropical island |
| concert | museum | zoo |
| farm | North Pole | _____ |
| fashion show | park | _____ |
| football game | pizza parlor | _____ |

First, we're greeted by Drummers
who drum as they come.
And next come the Strummers
who strum as they come.

# I'd like THESE instruments to be played at my party:

circle all the ones you'd like

| | | |
|---|---|---|
| accordion | guitar | saxophone |
| bagpipes | harmonica | sousaphone |
| banjo | harp | synthesizer |
| bassoon | harpsichord | tambourine |
| bongo | horn | triangle |
| bugle | kazoo | trombone |
| cello | lute | trumpet |
| clarinet | lyre | tuba |
| cornet | mandolin | ukulele |
| cymbals | maracas | viola |
| drums | oboe | violin |
| flügelhorn | organ | xylophone |
| flute | piano | zither |
| French horn | piccolo | _____ |
| glockenspiel | recorder | _____ |

Here comes your cake!
Cooked by Snookers and Snookers,
The Official Katroo
Happy Birthday Cake Cookers.

# I like cake.

YES ☐

NO ☐ (I like _____ better!)

# My **favorite** kind of **cake** is:

chocolate ☐

white ☐

yellow ☐

_____ ☐

# My **favorite frosting** is:

chocolate ☐

lemon ☐

strawberry ☐

vanilla ☐

_____ ☐

I decorated this cake

paste photo here

This is me blowing out the candles
on my REAL birthday cake

# Today you are you!
# That is truer than true!
# There is no one alive
# who is you-er than you!

## Some of my FAVORITE THINGS

(They make me *me-er* than anyone alive!)

My favorite animal _____

My favorite book _____

My favorite class at school _____

My favorite color _____

My favorite day of the week _____

My favorite dinosaur _____

My favorite food _____

My favorite friend _____

My favorite game _____

My favorite hobby _____

My favorite holiday _____

My favorite movie _____

My favorite place _____

My favorite planet _____

My favorite song _____

My favorite sport _____

My favorite subject _____

My favorite teacher _____

My favorite team _____

My favorite TV show _____

Shout loud,
"I am lucky to be what I am!
Thank goodness
I'm not just a clam or a ham!"

**I'M** lucky because

_____

_____

_____

_____

_____

# Clams and hams are
# NOT so lucky because

_____

_____

_____

_____

_____

"I am
what I am!
That's a great
thing to be!"

# I am ALL these things:

I AM _____Unique_____.

I AM _____.

I AM _____.

I AM _____.

I AM _____.

I AM _____.

I AM _____.

I AM _____.

"If I say so myself,
HAPPY BIRTHDAY TO ME!"

## My favorite birthday cards:

are funny ☐

are pretty ☐

have animals on them ☐

have cartoon characters
on them ☐

have presents inside! ☐

Now, by Horseback
and Bird-back
and Hiffer-back, too,
Come your friends!
All your friends!
From all over Katroo!

# I would like to spend my birthday with these friends and family members:

_____

_____

_____

_____

_____

_____

_____

And the Birthday Pal-alace
heats up with hot friends
And your party goes on!
On and on till it ends.

**I drew hands on this clock
to show when I want my party to START** ↙

**I drew hands on this clock
to show when I want my party to END**

I'm okay if it never ends! YES ☐ NO ☐

# I'd like to do these things on my FUTURE birthdays!

On my 13th birthday:

_____

On my 16th birthday:

_____

On my 25th birthday:

_____

On my 50th birthday:

_____

On my 75th birthday:

_____

On my 100th birthday:

_____

**I drew this picture of myself at age** _____

# So that's what the Birthday Bird
# Does in Katroo.
# And I wish I could do
# all these great things for you!

If I could do a great thing for someone, I would

_____

_____

for

_____ .

It would be great because

_____

_____

_____

_____

# Write a card to yourself!

Cut on dotted line, fold in half, color and decorate!

To, _____

_____

_____

_____

Love, _____

_____